BOSS GRADY'S BOYS

BOSS GRADY'S BOYS

Sebastian Barry

Raven Arts Press/Dublin

BOSS GRADY'S BOYS
is first published in 1989 by
THE RAVEN ARTS PRESS
P.O. Box 1430
Finglas
Dublin 11
Ireland.

ISBN 1 85186 059 2

Raven Arts Press receives financial assistance from The
Arts Council (An Chomhairle Ealaíon), Dublin, Ireland.

Designed by Dermot Bolger & Aidan Murphy.
Cover design by Susanne Linde.
Cover Photo by Fergus Bourke.
Printed and Bound in Ireland by Future Print Ltd., Dublin.

Boss Grady's Boys was first presented in Dublin at the Abbey Theatre (Peacock stage) on the 22nd August 1988 when the cast was as follows:

MICK .... *Jim Norton*
JOSEY .... *Eamon Kelly*
MRS MOLLOY .... *Maureen Toal*
MRS SWIFT .... *Máire O'Neill*
MR REAGAN .... *Gerard McSorley*
FATHER .... *Oliver Maguire*
MOTHER .... *Bríd Ní Neachtain*
GIRL .... *Gina Moxley*

The play was directed by Caroline Fitzgerald and designed by Carol Betera with lighting by Tony Wakefield. Costume design was by Carol Betera and Rachel Pigot-Judd. Music was by Thomas McLaughlin.

Characters

Mick Grady
Josey Grady
Mrs Molloy
Mrs Swift
Mr Reagan
Boss Grady *(Father)*
Mother
Girl
Four Dancers *(optional)*

The play is set on a forty-acre hill-farm on the Cork–Kerry border.

NOTES ON THE CHARACTERS

MICK *Sixties, small, slight. Hair still dark.*
JOSEY *Seventies, larger than his brother Mick, sandy-white hair.*
MRS MOLLOY *Sixties, ample.*
MRS SWIFT *Sixties, gray, trim.*
MR REAGAN *Sixties, meagre.*
FATHER *Boss Grady, medium height, stocky, bellied, in his sixties. Father of Mick and Josey.*
MOTHER *Late twenties, tallish, scraggy, long thin reddish face.*
GIRL *Eighteen, small, undernourished, unappealing, thin hair, almost bald.*

Permissions:
Curtis Brown,
162-168 Regent Street,
London W1R 5TB,
England.

NOTE ON THE FIRST PRODUCTION

I count myself extremely fortunate in the people that were gathered for the first production of Boss Grady's Boys. Caroline Fitzgerald the director, the players Oliver Maguire, Maureen Toal, Gerry McSorley, Máire O'Neill, Bríd Ní Neachtain, Gina Moxley and, as the brothers, Jim Norton and Eamon Kelly, have my deepest gratitude.

In the first production, the stage was arranged differently than printed here. The fireplace was a solid affair, and was positioned extreme right. The two windows in the text became one good-sized window upstage centre, on the ledge of which Josey had his 'kitchen'; there was a niche here also for the fiddle, which allowed Josey to use it in the final moments of Act Two, playfully, as a gun; the window was attached to the stairs, going up a little way to nowhere. The scenes, marked in the text by numbers, were connected during rehearsals by movements that fitted the existing dialogue; there were a few blackouts as a result. Also the window, stairs and fireplace were on stage from the start, and everything took place as it were in the house. In Act Two, 9, the threshold was considered as downstage centre, and the horse crossing was indicated by sound only.

In Act One, 9, the bed remained on stage, and was used for a horse, instead of one suggested by light. The dancers did not appear in Act Two, 3.

To everyone, Marie Kean, Thomas McLaughlin, Carol Betera, Tony Wakefield, Rachel Pigot-Judd, Michael Higgins, David Nolan and Kate Hyland; the Artistic Director of the Abbey, Vincent Dowling, and the Script Editor, Christopher Fitz-Simon; and the many people who worked to make the first production such an experience for the writer, heartfelt thanks.

A special thanks to Caroline Fitzgerald.

Sebastian Barry,
Dublin,
1989.

9

TO PHILIP CASEY

ACT I

ACT ONE

1

Curtain.

MICK sitting on the ground, slightly to left of centre, with a large purple sweep of light as of a mountain beyond him. He is a smallish figure, with a fishing hat on his head. He has his back to us, with his legs gripped in. It is evening, but early, and there is a full rich red in the sky above the mountain, which burns. The sky deepens and sweeps from right to left in a hurry. As a wind blows against his back he grips closer, keeping his head low, but watching the sunset. All around him is shadowy. The sky as it loses the sun gets deeper and deeper red, till it goes out. Then MICK is left in a dark-blue light obscuring the stage.

2

A tiny glimmer of light appears where the sun went and this increases to the dull glow of a turf fire. MICK is in the same spot, but turned three-quarters to us, on a stool, staring into the fire. He is wearing the same black working trousers, an old nylon shirt, but without his hat. His face is hard and neat, shaven, his hair blackish, trained back, cropped close.
JOSEY comes into the light from the other side, the right, pulling up a backed kitchen chair. JOSEY's hair is sandy-white, wavy but thinnish, a little too long. He wears brown working trousers, a whitish shirt, and a brown jacket. He has his cap in his hand, which he then settles on his head. He sits in his place, the fire between them.

JOSEY: I'd make tea for a halfpenny. Will I bring the horse down and put him closer to the house? I don't like the creature up there above the house in this rain.

13

MICK stares with his own thoughts into the fire.

JOSEY: I was thinking today all day there was likely to be a deal of rain later, and now it has held off till night-time. There's something in the weather that it's always the same. You can predict it after a fashion. Well, Mick? So.

MICK *(not looking at him):* There's just wind.

JOSEY: Is there no rain? Then the horse can talk to himself in peace. Will I call in the old dog so?

MICK *(looking up at him):* You old bastard. Can you not enjoy the fire?

JOSEY: The old dog will be cold. He has no good bones left. Every one of them is a nuisance to him. But he is a very lovable dog.

MICK: We've no dog now, Josey man. You buried him. He's up to his neck in soil, and I'm sorry for it. The sheep knew him well. It will trouble me to train a new one.

JOSEY: It was lovely how he lay in the grass with the sheep. He was such a big mess of black. The sheep loved him.

MICK: You fool. The sheep loved him? He never did lay down with the sheep.

JOSEY: No, Mick. I meant when you were steering them. I meant when you told him to go down, when you had them going right. Just how he dropped down, the big black fellow. Collapsed at your word. You see I enjoyed that. The sheep loved him.

MICK: The sheep didn't love him.

JOSEY: Well. He was very black and he lay in the grass. In the summer he looked well enough in the grass, when the grass was drier. Will I shout from the door for him?

14

MICK: Christ, man.

JOSEY: You have great whistles.

JOSEY stands, sticks his hands in his pockets, leans forwards. He gives a weak whistle, waves an arm. He gives two whistles, and laughs, and tries to whistle, calms, waves an arm.

MICK: Quiet yourself.

JOSEY: I'm driving the sheep into the slope field, because the grass there is perfect, perfect. Listen to me.

JOSEY whistles again, and calls:

Shep! Shep! Shep! Gubb-a-bubb-em! Down, down!

He is nearly weeping

MICK: Ah, man. You've just driven the sheep away up across the hill. The dog's died from contradiction.

JOSEY *(laughing)*: Bloody me! Aye, aye, aye.

He twirls himself, and makes a dance gesture, spreading out his hands, one foot out to the side, and holds it, and attempts a tap dance.

MICK: You're feeling your oats.

JOSEY: I am, heart. I am. Fred Astaire, man. I'm a great dancer. There will be a lady in a satin dress in here, if you don't stop me.

MICK *(savagely)*: Sit down and shut up.

JOSEY, chastened, settles his cap, and sits again. They both stare at the fire.

3

The same, but the fire is just a low ashen glow.

JOSEY *(leaning in)*: We would never go to Killarney now for the pictures, I suppose. Groucho Marx is a great man. The head of the country that time. *(Sings)* Hail Freedonia! Hail Freedonia! *(from the song in the Marx Brothers' Duck Soup)*. It was a lovely song. I loved the ducks in the pot, with the steam, but the ducks were alright. And that lovely woman with the big soft bosom. A soft night. A woman of a sort you won't see often in Bantry, unless she's a foreign woman staying in the big hotel. I would choose to marry ten women like that, and have them all in the loft stacked like big hayricks. We could lie on them and pray for help. The Yankee horses would come streaming up the track, with a pretty clatter, and rescue us.

MICK *(affectionately)*: You old fool, you.

JOSEY: Groucho, Harpo, Chico, and what's-his-name, and what was the name of the Frenchy man, the singer, on the boat with them that time?

MICK: You old blasted fool.

JOSEY: He was old in that picture, old but handsome, the perfect man for the bosomy lady.

MICK: You know, I remember his name. It was Maurice Chevalier.

JOSEY: What was his name, what was his name?

MICK looks at him, blinks slowly.

JOSEY: It's like wringing the necks of hens.

4

MICK is standing on a small wooden stairs, downstage right, shadowed. He is looking at JOSEY who is hunched over the embers of the fire. JOSEY has his hands outstretched to embrace the heat. There is a noise of waterdrops hissing in the embers.

JOSEY: The rain now. Coming in the same as October's rats from the cold. The horse will be a lonely man in the field. There'll be mud now on his hooves, and he has no fire or talk to protect him. Maybe I should have walked up in the cold and got him. He could stand outside the door here and listen to us. He could do so. It is like when Mick Collins was all the fashion, and Mick was away every night, and then every night away after that, when the old man was dead as a dog and the farm was ours in a way. It was our farm and no one came up the track to say otherwise. There were hens galore with brown eggs in them, there were two old pigs that wouldn't breed anymore, there were more sheep, and a milking cow to boot. It is like that now, as if Mick were away all night at his game, and the country very silent in its manner around me. It is like that, with a bat coming in from the dark and losing his way in the firelight. Mick away, and the dark roof moving with the firelight. Mick away. Little heat from the fire in this state, the moon in her own house, Collins the same man that was buried afterwards. He was a big black man with a greasy face. Mick told me. He was the king of the country in his time. He was a lonely sort of man, I suppose. And he made me lonely. I'd make tea for a halfpenny.

MICK: Josey, come to bed.

5

A marriage bed to the left, one side facing us. MICK is lying on it on his side, with his face towards us, eyes open. JOSEY is vaguer behind him, his face turned up to the ceiling can be seen. They are covered in worn army blankets with a faded coverlet on top. The sheets are flannelette, brownish, the pillow is the one bolster. MICK has a finger in his mouth. There is a bit of a candle lighting his face, but the space beside the end of the bed, which is ample, is empty and pitch. MICK's expression responds slightly to what JOSEY says.

JOSEY: A little bit of everything. A little bit of woe, a bit of mirth. A bit of bread, a bit of good butter. *(after a bit)* Bless you, and bless us in return. Bless this small house and bless me and Mick. Bless the sheep and the dog and the horse. Go up and talk to the horse in his field in your overcoat. Bless the piece of money in the bank in Killarney, if it's still there.

MICK throws his eyes quickly.

Bless the trees and the whins, and the rowanberries and the berries on them. Bless the rain and the rare sun and the seasons four. Bless the mam in heaven and the length of time since we seen her. Bless the gate and the slope field, and the rocky land at the top of the farm, which is no good to us. Bless our jackets and the few trousers and the shoes and the leather laces Mick bought this year. Bless the potatoes and the swedes and keep them whole and hale in their pit when the time comes to bury them in. That will be October. Bless the dog.

He pauses. MICK stares, waiting.

Bless. Bless. Bless. Bless the old man. Bless the turf. Bountiful Mary, come into us this night and bless us. Take your old blue cloak off for us, and God bless you, and bless the cups and the spoons, and bless the old fiddle ruined with damp, that the old man cherished as his own bride, and that is propped in the niche of the window. Bless the postman should he come, and bless the Bantry road, both to the town and to the mountain. Good night to you.

MICK wets his fingers and snuffs the candle.

JOSEY: Bless the darkness, come to that.

6 *Mick's Dream*

The bed very dimly seen, with two masks in place of the two men's faces. To the right of this, in the clear space, is a table with four people playing cards. An oil-lamp behind them gives the light. This, starting from nothing, is becoming brighter as the figures animate, then the scene darkens again. After a second or two the scene returns with the lamp fully lit, and exactly as the light is established, one of the two widows speaks. These are the widows of shopkeepers in Bantry. The other man is a widower, a shopkeeper himself.

MRS MOLLOY: What is it about cards that makes you thirsty? Is it the excitement?

She means this sarcastically. They are playing poker. MRS SWIFT can not make up her mind.

MRS SWIFT: Hold up a minute, dear. Just let a girl think. There's a cabinet of alchohol behind you, if you want it.

MRS MOLLOY: I wouldn't dream, I wouldn't dream.

MRS SWIFT: You don't want me to get it for you?

MRS MOLLOY: Would you stop, and ask Mr Reagan for your cards. You're making a very long job of it.

MR REAGAN: Two or three?

MRS SWIFT: I don't know. What do you think?

MR REAGAN: Don't show me! This is a game for profit, Mrs Swift. Have a heart.

MRS MOLLOY: Mr Grady?

MICK *(surprised in his thoughts):* No.

MRS MOLLOY: What do you mean, no?

MICK: Were you not asking me if I wanted a drink?

MRS MOLLOY: Man, you are worse than she is.

MRS SWIFT: There's whiskey behind you all in the cabinet. Dear me - two cards, please, Mr Reagan.

MICK: I'll have the four. I can do nothing with these.

MRS MOLLOY: Keep your cards close to your chest, Mr Grady, and a poker face. I hope you have that ace.

MICK: I need an ace?

MRS MOLLOY: To get four cards again you do.

MICK: Well, I have it of course. *(pleasantly)* Do you want to examine it?

MRS MOLLOY: Examine it? Keep it to yourself. I am indifferent to it.

MICK: What sort of whiskey, Mrs Swift? Irish?

MRS SWIFT: Not at all. Good scotch.

MICK: As I feared, as I feared.

MRS MOLLOY *(standing)*: As I feared, as I feared. A life of romance was the least a girl should expect. It was a good life in a way, but his shop was a mean shop, and there were too many items from India. He took away every year I had to give a man, and then took away himself for good measure. He was a man after my own heart so I will not blame him. *(sitting)* This is a tedious game after a while. It is not really a lady's game.

MR REAGAN: What is a lady's game in effect? Bridge?

MRS MOLLOY: That is a fine lady's game. But I can not play it.

MRS SWIFT: It needs brains. I can't play it either. It's a rich person's game.

MRS MOLLOY: There is often something very feeble and silly about you, Mrs Swift.

MRS SWIFT: Did you want that drink now, Mrs Molloy? I realise you want one.

MRS MOLLOY *(standing, to herself):* I wanted one, I did want one. Curly things the same as bees. I think woods are glad of bees, the babies of woods. I wanted a little son I could watch all his first years, and hear talk, and he could have gone to school and come home, simply, richly. I wanted a head to stroke, a head of hair, black hair. There is something about a boy of nine that is preferable to a girl. He looks at the world with innocence, but is a creature to take his place in it all the same, a king. Whereas, alas, as I know myself, the life of a girl is just the dickens. Every man in the street will touch you or look at you, and in the lanes among the bread-and-cheese bushes, when the May is on the branches, and the bees idle like engines, and the big cars ease through the mid-morning, someone will come thrashing through the nettles and the docks over the ditch, and drag you into a quiet glade and yank up your skirt and murder his joke into you. A girl of nine should not go out walking in an Irish lane, when the May is out. *(sits)*

MICK: Are you going to give me four, Eamon?

MR REAGAN: Are you innocent of them? Sorry. *(He gives MICK four new cards)* A bit of butter, a bit of bread. Fresh from Killarney. Comes in at six, you know, around the new coast road. We call it the new road because heretofore we were not in contact with the mainland, as we dubbed it, though we are not an island. My wife, usually a well woman, is buried some while since. We sell the Press, the Independent and the Examiner, but not the Irish Times. Though this is a planter town, which you might not expect so far south, we don't stock the Irish Times as a rule. There is very little reading in it, unless you are a Dublin man, or gentry. There are no gentry in this district, nor has been for many a long decade. We got rid of them quite. We burned them out. They were glad to leave and, indeed, we have baking powder, and custard, and even oats if you wanted them for your porridge. Every brand name you can think of lives in here a merry merry life.

MRS SWIFT: I have a right bellyache from that chicken. What can Dempsey's be thinking of, stocking chicken as tough as boots? I had to boil it for two days. Which included two nights. I heard it in the pantry, bubbling away in the heart of the old house. How very pretty my rooms look in the sunlight, in the night-time I often think they are a little tomblike, a little less than decent. My missal however keeps me going. There are some lovely prayers in the missal. Don't you often think that, Mrs Molloy? But I doubt if you would, with your roly-poly body and happy air and attraction to men. But if you asked my opinion, in a month of Sundays, your face is the visage of a horse, with a touch of hair where hair ought not to be on a woman. But never mind, have another piece of gateau. This is fresh gateau from Killarney and Mr Reagan's shopeen. It looks like the flesh of an old man's belly, my nice old man who never laid a hand on me without his mass-gloves on. I can not abide, or could not in the days when Declan was still living, the touch of a living man's hand on my person. It gave me the chills, such as was not to be countenanced. And yet, in the happy cinema in Killarney years ago, it was a different matter were a youth such as, well, whoever he might be, to just for a moment, just for a moment, well, fondle me. *(clearing her throat)* I wouldn't be seen dead in the street without my foundation and face-powder, though I understand from the younger set that powder has gone out of fashion. I like the puff and the case in my handbag always. I suppose they don't wear stays either. But some people are ill-advised not to wear stays. The trees in the little square stay firm even in old age, but we, well, really, it's obvious.

MICK: I've nothing.

MRS MOLLOY: Everything comes to him who waits. Don't be a girl ever in a boy's world. Last winter I went out in the yard with a pan of cinders and threw them glowing on the snow.

MR REAGAN: Are we playing cards or what? I don't mean to pry. Tomorrow I may go out from the town for good and become a countryman proper. Set up on a hill farm like Mick and his brother, and be simple. I can then be in a position to walk to the town from the farm and back again, through light rain, and will be especially excited by the numerous murmurings of small chaffinches and robins and sparrows. A light fiddle-music, giving rise to the traditional music. I'd rather be done with it here than endure another odd night above in Crow Street in my little room.

MRS SWIFT: Well, come to that, I might put on every inch of good stuff I have, and go out on the Killarney road and be taken in by some traveller - commercial but not tinker. It really is a bonus not having to submit to gentle entreaties. I much prefer the greatness of our air, the famous Irish air that the foreigners love. I am glad we can be so giving to the foreigners, with our air. The foreigners are very fine people, very fine. They came from all over.

MICK: We appear to be stuck with this hand. Will we play something else?

MRS MOLLOY (standing, putting her leg up on the table, showing a garter): We could play house. That's a good game.

MICK: It's not a card game though, you know.

MRS MOLLOY: There's something I've always liked about you, Mick Grady. You may be a small wizened little creature with a square face and dark skin denoting I don't know what, but you have an advantage, a steal on other men in these parts. I am a very soft person, you know, that might be sunk into, with profit. (she sits)

MICK: Rightyo, rightyo. Time to go home. Time to go home. Josey will still be up.

MR REAGAN: How is your brother, Mick? Is he in good fettle.

MICK: He is. But he is also a man that feels loneliness very keenly, and begins to pine if I'm away long. He forgets to make tea for himself, or cannot do it if I am not at home. He is a very peculiar, unnecessary brother that I have come to revere and value by hook and by crook.

MR REAGAN: Is your brother well, Mick?

MICK: My brother is a well, deep, stony and dry. I throw stones into the poor man that echo with a lost, deep sort of echo. I love him, I love his idiocy.

MICK turns about, and kneels on his chair, turned from the others, facing upstage left. Two high columns of variously coloured light like stained-glass windows appear, strengthen, displacing the other scene. Light falls through the windows onto MICK.

MICK: Lord of the streams, the hills, the farms, of the farmers, what's wrong with us, what's amiss with us? I'm a smallish man. I would like a slightly larger acreage, with a deal of sunlight to improve the grazing. I don't actually. *(to himself)* I won't talk to glass windows any more. I won't go along with them. Let the old women do it. Old bastes, old cattle, I won't have a word for them any more. It's idle little, idle little. On my knees in front of windows. On my knees as if He was an English lord. If He met me on the road in his car He would spit through the side-window at me. Long ago in his pony-and-trap He would have leant out with His whip, and stroked me with it. Down on my knees.

He stretches out his arms.

Away up the road with you, you foreigner you!

Windows disappear, lamp-light returns, MICK sits as before.

MR REAGAN: We never see your brother in the town now. Is he well? We went to the same school and we never see him now. He was a great fellow for catching wrens. He had the knack. He could catch a wren nimbly with lime on a stick and he might weep for it after, but what can you do?

MICK: With all my red heart I wish he might not survive

me alone in the house. And yet I wish that I might not survive him. I will not live here with his shadow and our father's shadow, and I expect I will. They would certainly not leave him be, if they ever saw him do what I see him do. He is a brother that many people would be glad to know. A diverse brother but a comfortable one. He would never get in your way willingly or knowingly.

MRS MOLLOY: I suppose people say odd things about me. I am bothered by the thought. I always like to be liked where possible. Of course I am a dryish woman, an empty sort. There was a deal of love in me at one time. Someone to caress me.

MICK: Well, there's my hand *(putting down the cards)*.

MR REAGAN: Is there no more betting? I suppose not if you've shown. You have three kings and a pair of tens. That's enough to lick me.

MRS SWIFT: I had only a number of very different cards. I've no luck tonight.

MR REAGAN: There's no real need to say what you had if you don't wish, I believe.

MRS SWIFT: I don't mind telling you. I wanted to. All through the game I felt a little foolish, holding such cards, and betting pennies on them.

MRS MOLLOY *(looking at her, almost kindly)*: You ought to have stopped, Mrs Swift. Don't you know you can stop?

MRS SWIFT: Of course.

Lamp fades.

7   *Josey's dream.*

The bed, as before. In the clear space on the right it is blueish, misty, with a sparkling of light from the ground to the extreme right, where water is. A middle-sized,

25

thick-set man with wavy white hair, in his sixties, dressed in workclothes, comes carefully from the left carrying a fishing-rod and a bundle of line whose hooks have cork stuck on the tips, a round float at the end. It is stormy.

FATHER: It has to be a storm inside a mist.

JOSEY: *(offstage left):* Dad! Have I lost my way? Am I right for the lake?

FATHER: A curious thing that the storm takes his words and carries them to me. *(he puts down the line at the water's edge and arranges and then casts his fly-rod).* If I catch a trout in this wind I will know a great deal. But it has to be a storm inside a mist.

JOSEY *(coming on muddily):* I never trust that path.

FATHER: There's no path that I know of.

JOSEY: I've crossed it a few times and I don't still believe it will take me.

FATHER *(nodding at the lake):* What do you think?

JOSEY: There are crazy fish in there today.

FATHER: They'd always be in there, Josey. It's a lake.

JOSEY: Well, I can smell them, I can smell them!

FATHER: Then you have a fine nose. I have only mist in mine. It's funny that we come up here, the only lake in Cork or Kerry that needs a storm, in a place that has no road after the mountain road, and where the trout are the wildest buggers alive. You need to be a genius to catch these trout, and in a storm at that.

JOSEY: The storm makes them hungry.

FATHER: I expect so. It is called Hungry Hill.

JOSEY: There are many big trout under the waves today, Dad. Are we to throw out the line?

FATHER: If we catch one on the rod, we'll throw the line out. We'll try the line if we catch one now. *(working the rod)*.

JOSEY: There is something fierce about the fish up here. Isn't there a very wicked look to them, to their jaws? Do you remember when you brought me up here with the other men, and you made a line with fifty hooks, and stood both sides of the lake and walked its length? And you got as many as thirty fish, each one bigger and wickeder than the last.

FATHER: I don't. I don't remember.

JOSEY: There was a blue colour at the top of the sky, a strange blue colour like it was hot, and the fog was clothy and bright, and the edges of the grass tufts gleamed at the light. You and the men shouted across the water to each other, and it was a very bright storm with lights. It was very exciting.

FATHER: No. I don't recall that.

JOSEY: I was very young at the time. Perhaps that is why. It is hard to remember when you are very young.

FATHER: There are no fish in here today I think.

JOSEY: There must be. Fish away.

FATHER: No, there are none. It's not likely you'll get one if you don't get one straight away.

JOSEY: It is such a long walk. Fish away.

FATHER: No, it will be better if we go down. We're wasting our time. Maybe the wind is in the worse direction.

JOSEY: Stay, Dad. Fish!

FATHER *(turning to Josey):* Be quiet and silent, you cretin, can't you? There are no fish if I say so.

JOSEY: Dad, be gentle with me. I am very excited and eager to see a fish.

FATHER: Christ, do you not hear me? Will you not back away? Will you not go some distance there? Would you block my path?

JOSEY: Fish away, Dad, fish away.

FATHER: I'd rather crush you. I'd rather put my hands each side of your soft brain and pancake it. Do you think I want you running up here with me like a collie, a foolish collie that won't herd sheep without biting them? What class of a shitty boy are you? Will you not give me peace?

JOSEY: We were up this morning at four, before even the night was gone. It was only morning by courtesy. You gave me bran and beer to drink, and we tied the rod and the line to your bicycle, and went off down the lane to the road. We have walked and ridden, me on the crossbar, for two hours, and now it is nearly daylight outside the storm. All night I was awake in the loft with Mick, breathing under the close wood, hot and shaking. I was going to fish with my father in the morning and we are here now. You did not take Mick.

FATHER: I will kill you here. I have killed sheep in their flocks and flocks, and chickens' necks in their thousands, and I have swiped at rats in the sheds, and cut them in two with the spade. I have crushed more spiders in my time than a bird has cracked snail-shells. Do you think it would be a great thing for me to crush you? You are small and weak-headed.

JOSEY: Dad, I am old and weak-headed. My hair is grey as yours. You lay on the threshold of the house like a flounder, staring up at Mick as he leaned over you in astonishment. You looked at him with your fish's eyes, and your heart stopped budging in your chest. And you never took Mick to fish, and he often asked me why was that.

FATHER: You were my favourite, Josey. You were like a daughter to me. You were a lovely faithful daughter, as good as a dog. You honoured me. You were too stupid to look at me the way Mick did. You were too doltish to question. You were the half of me I preferred, you'd no brain to mar you. I wish I had been born like you, without a real thought in my head. You were the best half of me, the half of me I killed in myself always. Mick was the most familiar section of me. He could see me through and through.

Light gathers and moves around the father.

JOSEY *(hunched, quietly, speaking to the ground):* Fish away, Dad, fish away.

8

The bed, as before. The space to the extreme right has a bright hard sunlight. MICK is standing exteme right, leaning into the fall of the light, hands in trouser pockets, in his Sunday best: clean shirt, checked, with green tie, good jacket, a newer fishing hat with a small feather, all his clothes a little tight for him. He says nothing for the moment, while the following lighting changes take place: the sunlight persists for some seconds, then gradually a cloud goes over, shadowing the space inch by inch. A wind gusts at MICK, the sunlight edges back, and a glittering light rain falls in the same direction as the light falls. MICK does not move out of it. He leans into the sun-shower.

MICK *(in a quiet mumble, it is a line from the a Marx Brothers film):* Room Service? Room Service? *(after a moment)* Send me up a room.

His head dips an inch, and he cries with open eyes, not caring in the rain. After some seconds he is able to stop crying.

I was eager for them all, and at the same time didn't care much for them. It was the way Collins looked, the way he stared about him like a tiger, that I admired. Not the politics. Or it was the politics. It was the politics, certainly, but I suspected it was always going to be the spirit of the times that I and my like would remain where we were and make do with that. In the rain and the cow's muck, and the companionship of a softheaded brother. Whiskey with a glow, and the brother-warm bed. You can strive, you can talk hard in a bar at night, and you want it to mean something, you have a few ideas how things might go when the business is done. What to set up and what to avoid, who to allow and who to resist, who is the mean man in the town and who the generous helper, the man with no thought for himself, who would lead best, and make decisions that would spruce up the farms and the feeling of the farmers. So there wouldn't be a burden ever again, or any loss, or any misdemeanour. That we wouldn't be fodder for books again, that we wouldn't be called peasants in a rural district, and be slipped into the role of joker by the foreigners from the cities. That we wouldn't have to stand on the roadside and watch the cars go by with creatures in them from outer space, plastic and cushions and clothes, another Ireland altogether, not people who would mock our talk, and not see us, not talk to us except by way of favour. That we could be men of our country was all my wish, that we might have a country that would nurture us, a spirit to get us up the road and out of the rain. How is it that after every change and adjustment I still stand here in the same rain on the same mud, with the same sun laughing at me? And there's the time I stood in a bar with Mick Collins and told him we had the same name, and he said I seemed a very sound man, and thanked me for my part in the business. I said I would burn anything for him, shoot anyone, if we might have a nation after, a nation I would be a citizen of, an honoured ordinary man. And the world would hear of us, and wish to be near us. I said I would do the worst thing for him, if I might always wear my Sunday clothes and drive in a decent fashion over the roads, and get the damp out of my bones and he put his hands on my back as he was leaving and said he needed more men like me. Then he went off to his wars and I went back to the cardgame in the little room and never said a word about him to the others. I was moved beyond telling them, I was aflame from my toes up my legs, it was a real feeling. I was going to walk across the fields with my legs on fire and walk over everything that was beating me down and set it aflame: my father would smile on the hearth and laugh at me in a different way than the sun: he would honour me. Then I would go out with his spade and a bit of cement and build up everything again, and put the good man in a big house, and leave the mean man to himself. There was a lot to be done. Now the good man I had my eye on is a man on his own in the neighbouring farm, with a bicycle for vehicle and a mossy house, and his sole adventure is the shopping trip to Bantry on a Tuesday. I was to make everything watertight for Collins, and be a decent man in my own district. I was never, myself, to stand carelessly in the rain again. I was to be a dry man with responsibilities.

9

The bed gone. Outside the house. Dull overcast light for the main part, now and then a sweep of sunlight passes from right to left. MICK is sorting tools in a toolbox, humming. The sound of hooves walking on clattering stones is heard, at which MICK stands straight and watches. JOSEY comes on from the right, leading a 'horse'. Aspects of the horse are suggested by light. JOSEY responds to its movements: his hands go up and he admonishes the horse when it chucks its head. It is a big animal. JOSEY stops and pulls on the unseen rope.

JOSEY: Hup,hup.

He walks, and brings up the animal to where MICK is. MICK backs away when the horse pushes its flank against him. MICK smooths the horse's nose and the horse pushes against his hand, and MICK laughs.

JOSEY: Stand now, Charlie, stand.

MICK: Go back there *(pushing his flank)*. Go back.

JOSEY: Is he to stand or go back?

31

MICK: Hold him steady by the halter.

JOSEY: Is he looking well to you?

MICK: He looks fine.

JOSEY: He does too, the creature.

MICK: How's the grass up there?

JOSEY: Not great at that. A bit sparse. He has more mud made under the rowanberries than a herd of bullocks.

MICK: Poor old fellow, poor old fellow.

He strokes the horse's big neck and slaps it. These sounds, the patting, the horse shifting his hooves on the rocky ground, are heard. The horse snorts heavily.

JOSEY: Oh, the man. Would we be as well to do his mane? It's very knotted.

MICK: He's a lovely big girl.

JOSEY:A big girl? This great gelding?

MICK: What was the farrier's name, that used to come?

JOSEY: Driscoll. The songwriter.

MICK: Hold him now, and I'll pare him.

He bends down at the near hind, and tries to pull up the hoof, facing away from the animal, aiming to draw the leg up between his own legs.

MICK: Come on.

JOSEY: Raise it up, raise it up. Charlie knows you're only a tailor.

MICK struggles with the leg, and gets it resting on his thigh. With a pliers from the box he pulls the 'nails' of the loose 'shoe' and prises the 'shoe' off and throws the pliers (as if with the shoes and nails) back in the box with a clatter. He takes the parer and cuts some of the 'hoof'.

MICK: Do you want to give me that new shoe? Give me a mouth of nails.

JOSEY hands him a shoe and some nails from a pocket of his jacket, and Mick puts the nails in his mouth, five, that jut out. MICK fits the shoe against the pared 'surface' (his hand holds the shoe the necessary distance from his thighs) and pares some more. The horse forces his leg down and moves forward a bit, going sideways.

MICK: Hold up, can't you.

JOSEY: He's a devil for that.

MICK: He's a rogue. Come on up now, Charlie.

MICK bends again and takes up the hoof and leg and puts the shoe against the 'hoof'. He takes a nail from his mouth and takes up the hammer and beats in the first nail, and does this with the other nails with a rhythmical tapping. The horse snorts loudly.

MICK: Keep him steady now, Josey. *(throwing the hammer in the box, dipping for a file, filing off the hoof. The sound of this is heard).*

JOSEY: Steady now, stand.

MICK: Rightyo *(dropping the 'hoof' and stepping away, throwing the file in the box, with the shoe and its nails at the same time).* Is the lower gate hasped?

JOSEY: Aye.

MICK: We can let him be here then. He'll be safe enough.

JOSEY takes off the invisible halter with some effort, because the horse holds his head high. The sound of the horse walking away calmly, and snorting again.

MICK: Fine so. The other feet are fine?

JOSEY: Ah sure yes.

MICK: Sound. Tea, so. He has slain me.

10

Outside. More overcast, darker with the threat of rain, slatey. JOSEY is standing left of centre, more downstage than MICK, who is standing idly. JOSEY is looking up at the sky, facing us.

MICK: *(Singing vaguely and softly, suddenly)*: Hoot en night en noot en night en noot en night en nyah.

(JOSEY shakes his head slowly at the sky.)

MICK *(suddenly again)*: Hoot en night en noot en night en noot en nyah.

JOSEY *(suddenly, after a bit, looking up still)*: It smells like vultures.

MICK *(turning away, walking upstage, light going)*: Come on, JOSEY.

JOSEY after a bit follows him. As they move upstage, curtain falls.

ACT II

ACT TWO

1

The kitchen. MICK on his kness putting a match to the fire. The light increases slowly during the next few minutes of talk, finishing at the full glow of the fire. Noise of hard heavy rain falling outside.

MICK: That'll be it now for the whole of October, and November too maybe.

JOSEY *(right, in the shadows):* Cheese and bread I'm making.

MICK: As long as you make tea I don't mind what I eat. I've no taste left much.

JOSEY: I stood on the road this late evening and Brady talked to me. He said the boy in the top farm -

MICK: What boy?

JOSEY: Away up there where the waterfall is, and the mountain meadow — we were up there as lads. It is full of black pools. I remember it. There's a farm under the lot.

MICK: Of course there is. *(rising)* You mean Jack Dillon's place.

JOSEY: Well, he's dead.

MICK: Jack?

JOSEY: He died in the county hospital. He was in for a stomach complaint and got a pneumonia while he was there. Off he went.

MICK: He was afraid of the hospital. He used to shovel

stomach powders into himself. I saw as many as a score of empty tins in his parlour. *(sitting on his stool, left)* His mother was dead a long time.

JOSEY: Brady said it was a sudden affair.

MICK: He'd know.

JOSEY: Will you go down to Killarney for the funeral?

MICK: I won't.

Flash of lightning, illuming the left window.

JOSEY: They wouldn't be expecting you.

MICK: Give me that bread, will you? He had no one.

JOSEY comes to the fire, and hands him a saucer of sandwiches, and a cup.

MICK: Grub.

Thunder outside.

JOSEY: I didn't see the flash.

MICK: You were cutting cheese, man.

JOSEY: Peeling it off, anyway. The wood will be soaked.

MICK: It will be burned. I stacked it in. The turf's good though. We weren't cheated.

JOSEY: Is that our turf?

MICK: It's Carney's. I didn't dig a sod this year. My foot is banjaxed all summer.

JOSEY: It's a poor thing when we burn someone else's turf. Did you pay money for it?

MICK: I did not. He owed me many a favour. Don't you

remember that great long week spent putting up his wire fencing?

JOSEY: Was I with ye?

MICK *(laughing):* As far as I knew.

JOSEY: Well, there now.

MICK: Sit, can't you?

JOSEY: I'll call in the dog.

MICK *(quickly):* Don't start that.

JOSEY: Is the father in?

MICK: Don't start that either. I won't stand it. I'll have to go out.

JOSEY *(turning away to the shadows, right):* I suppose he's caught at the fair. Why did we bring no sheep to the fair this time?

MICK: It's not fair day, is why. I have two ewes I want to sell on that day. I am sick of looking at them. They'll never be lambs in those ewes. They're only shadows of sheep. They're just grass-eaters.

JOSEY: Would they stew?

MICK: If you had a year spare to boil them.

JOSEY: Well, so, I'd sell them quietly.

MICK: Some of them half-wit farmers from Kenmare might go for them.

JOSEY: Why not? They're grand sheep.

MICK: Are you eating over there in the dark? The fire's warm now. *(after a bit)* Bring your chair over here can't you, man dear.

JOSEY: Where's that father at all? *(coming over with his chair, and a cup)*

MICK: Did you eat?

JOSEY: What's eating? I've no hunger. *(looking into Mick's cup)* You have cinders splashed on it.

MICK: I raised the ashes when I swept. You need fuelling, man.

JOSEY: Eat yourself. Go on.

MICK: I will. *(Josey sits)* That's a terrible rain. We'll be stuck with it now for a month. We'll be like fish in here now for a month.

JOSEY: The wood will be very wet.

MICK: I stacked it, heart. *(Josey gets up)* What's troubling you?

JOSEY: I'm going to piss.

A bright green light, and yellow light, as if a hedgerow, appears in front of Josey. He stands in the midst of this light. A young GIRL with very thin poor hair and ill-dressed, rickety and frail and scrawny as a hen, approaches. JOSEY ducks back. The girl looks morose, off-putting, and sick. JOSEY holds out his arm at her and smiles. Rook noises. The GIRL does nothing, does not look at him. JOSEY jumps at her and flattens her on the ground, noiselessly, and rolls off. The GIRL gets up and walks on. Lighting returns to kitchen as before.

MICK: What happened to you?

JOSEY: I tripped on the linoleum.

MICK *(getting up and helping him)*: You poor old sod. Have you pulled anything?

JOSEY: I've not pulled the hernia anyway. I must be

alright. I don't feel anything.

MICK: It's not good for an old man to fall. You'll have arthritis on the bumps for Christmas. *(laughs)*

JOSEY: I'm a very clumsy sort of man, I expect.

MICK: You're not. You're a dancer. A real dancer. Catch your breath.

JOSEY: God bless me, I've pissed.

MICK: You shocked yourself. You confused yourself.

JOSEY: I hate that. All wet. *(he shakes his trousers a little)* Tch, a poor excuse.

MICK: Wear your Sunday.

JOSEY *(astonished):* On a Monday? Are you ill? I'll put on the old brown jobs.

MICK: Josey, boy, you have more holes in them than a cloth. They're a walking disgrace.

JOSEY: They're dry though. I'll have a rash on me if I linger now.

MICK: Take them off, take them off, I'll get my other pair for you.

JOSEY: Oh, that will be grand. I like those trews. They have a kind of shine to them.

MICK: From sitting on my arse by the heat.

JOSEY laughs with his head back, very strangely.

2

MICK standing at the dark rectangle of the left window, suggested by gray-blue light. The window is quite big, a front window of a circa 1910 farmhouse. JOSEY is sitting

41

by the glow of the fire, sunk into the heat.

MICK: It is in spate, the river. It is a dangerous thing for Brady's cattle. Fools of people. *(after a bit, shaking his head)* Jack Dillon's waterfall, a wonder after rain. It was full of salmon once, that big stream. Pigfarmers! *(after a bit)* You sold them in scores to the Commercial Hotel, formerly. *(after a bit)* You wouldn't know what a flood would raise. I can't eat a salmon. Why would I?

JOSEY: *(vaguely, low as if it is a formula):* He has left us in our place, that man.

MICK: I wonder now, I wonder.

JOSEY *(low):* I never touched a woman in my born days. I'll sit inside this downpour forever.

MICK *(not looking back, but addressing Josey):* Do you want to start marrying someone? Where would you seat her? This farm would not divide. It is already a scrap.

Whinny of the horse outside, and a fall of light as he passes the window. His shape can be made out.

The big soft girl.

JOSEY: But I never touched a girl, unless you count the lass I knocked down in the lane.

MICK: If you don't knock them down, they won't lie down at all.

JOSEY: You never did it. It makes a man strange to himself. It is more breaking bones in a sack to add them to pigfeed, than any other thing.

MICK: If you don't knock them down, they won't lie down at all. The people in this valley are very silent. Just as well, sometimes. *(after a bit)* The roads will be streaming. *(after a bit)* The people in this valley are as far away from each other as old ships in a fog in an old sea-story. There's a fog of rain that keeps them apart. Only the fiddles kept any sort of company going. *(after a bit)* TV aerials.

JOSEY: If he ever had any thought of vengeance, he has it now certainly.

MICK: He has. *(after a bit)* Except we are like married people. We sleep in the same bed like the wed. It is like a marriage. *(after a bit)* Did he plan that, I wonder, him who seemed to despise mam's company while she breathed? When she was dead, he mourned her, tilled her plot like a little field, sowed it with a harvest of snowdrops. You'd think she had been a fine film-star.

JOSEY: Hail Freedonia!

MICK: A woman in ermine, stepping along in black and white, with a glister of moonlight on a Californian bay, and a dead man sunk under the jetty. Is that what he aimed at for us, a little marriage for her sake? Didn't I plot and plan to go to New York, where the tailoring would have been a good profession, instead of jobbing down there in the town for forty years, making jackets for the lunatics in the asylum, such jackets that hitched their arms, making them swing, putting a true mark of madness on the poor men. I made madmen mad-looking in my time. *(after a bit)* I sleep in his dip.

JOSEY: But why vengeance on myself? I was his favourite.

MICK: Josey, it was vengeance on me only.

JOSEY: You think I can sit here like an old gaslamp in peace?

MICK: No other peace would've suited your temperament, man.

JOSEY: I'd like to tell you, I had high hopes once, sitting in the flea-pit at Killarney, of going west myself in a train, feeding the carriages into the engine, and arriving in due time. I had no other hope in life than to be a Marx brother, a worthy ambition I should think.

43

MICK: It was. You should have had your chance, Josey, instead of being stuck here on a hill farm with me.

JOSEY: Aye.

MICK *(quietly):* That I might find the big scissors that would cut this farm in two. That I might eat my way through the sheep, and go to some glittery big city, with long cars in it.

JOSEY: Aye, and injuns, and wagons, and those big open farms with grass waving on them for days.

MICK: And drink at a distant bar, after work, and go home with a confident step, and put meat on the table in a brown parcel for my wife, who would be old now but pretty with make-up, like Mrs Molloy. To think that the girl I would have met, in some park or in some street, is now an old one like myself, and it was someone else she met and kissed, and was nervous talking to, and then grew stronger with. And all these years of seasons and floods, of greenery and streams and mud and whiskey nights, she has cleaned her American home, and looked out at the brisk sunlight without me.

JOSEY: I always wanted one of them furcoats, the sort that makes the head look like a lost moon, Mick, and a pair of them shining socks. I'd look like a scarecrow in them, but I could be happy in such attire. I might walk the length of the towns, and print my footstep in concrete like Charlie Chaplin, laughing with a jerk at me in the cinema. Now how did he know I was there to see him, to give me that laugh?

MICK: He gave it to us both.

JOSEY: I was always very like that boy that roomed with Charlie Chaplin. I might have been the boy.

MICK: You were the boy. You were always the boy. And you always wore a furcoat too, in effect.

JOSEY: *(after a bit)* He foxed us for fillies, God's truth.

44

3

Rain as before. JOSEY in the chair still. MICK is warming his hands and back at the fire near him. When he speaks he almost hisses.

MICK: Strange black hair, long red face, hard hands, good at shelling peas, soft lap enough, not a local woman, TB — Mam.

JOSEY: Rightyo...Mam.

MICK: Is that how you recall it?

JOSEY: I don't recall anything about it at all.

MICK: She kept hens there, in that very yard, such hens as few wouldn't want to own for themselves. She had three dresses, Mam, one black for deaths, one blue with white dots for wear, and a grey one for music. There were no bought clothes then, not up here.

JOSEY: Was she fair?

MICK: Listen to me. She was red-faced, black-haired. She couldn't speak a word of English or any other tongue.

JOSEY: Was that the way?

MICK: She kept her own counsel to the last degree. *(after a bit)* Silent all her life, except for peculiar grunts. She waved her arms a deal. When she shelled peas, she used a tin dish for them, and had a flick in her wrist that sent each row of peas in hard, with a kind of pattern. She could do it with my head on her lap. I watched the sky, and ting, ting, ting, went the peas behind my ears. I could hear her smiling. You have to get on with things. *(after a bit)* Thirty years old. If I saw her on the road now she'd look like a child. She was a great beauty, I should imagine. *(after a bit)* No. *(after a bit)* She could walk of course, and listen. She could hear the rain begin to fall over Bantry, seven miles away. She'd have the sheets in off the bushes in a twinkle, you wouldn't know why. The rain would be along presently. That's a talent.

JOSEY rises, and goes to the smaller window on the right, where the old fiddle is.

She scolded us with her hand. She seemed to make a favourite of me, I think. I appreciated it. But she didn't scorn you, nor neglected to tend to you, Josey. You were a wild boy often. You could throw a fit quicker than a rook in a tree of rooks. You were often a very wild rook, boy.

Rook noises. JOSEY comes back with the fiddle and its bow.

JOSEY: Listen to me now. I'll make it talk anyhow.

He plays the untuned strings, a scraping with the occasional note.

MICK *(in a gap in the playing):* Good. Lamentable but good. *(after a bit)* Good man, Josey.

Stage darkens. Four figures dance slightly, with their backs to us from the right, in a line. They are wearing cloaks at the back. JOSEY has his eyes closed in the murk. He plays on. The dancers turn briefly, with the same step in unison that Josey did earlier, splaying one hand, putting forward one foot. On this side they are wearing the costumes of chorusline dancers, glittery. They are large women. This happens briefly, then they turn their backs again, and dance off. Light as before.

MICK *(after JOSEY stops):* I don't know what the hell the tune was, but it put me in mind of something. How she was always very mouselike when he played. A great big woman like that.

JOSEY: I don't have the name of the tune.

MICK: It was a great pity.

JOSEY: I never had it.

MICK: No, that she was dumb. She was the kind of person you wanted to apply to for answers on certain matters. She had an awful clever look to her often.

JOSEY: I expect.

4

JOSEY is now asleep on the chair. MICK is over to the right, where a smaller smudge of windowlight is, the dark glimmer of a small window on the weather side of the farmhouse, where the fiddle is kept. He holds the fiddle in his hands, looking at it.

MICK: If you can play this you can do a lot. It has strings like Charlie's tail, very wisps of music, a music that has died in my hands and Josey's. There were tunes in this fox-coloured thing that would . . . When our legs were spindles in the school trousers we danced to his tunes, like fools of lambs. What's this silent tune we dance to now, the rain's hammers?

MICK stays quiet in the shadows. A patch of light shows the MOTHER in a blue and white dress, with a bowl and a few pods of peas. She is sitting downstage left. As she shells each pod deftly, she aims the peas into the bowl, where they rattle. She hums a tune silently, almost angrily. She gathers herself and gets up and carries the bowl and the empty pods over to the right, the light going with her as if a private atmosphere, to where MICK stood before in the rain. MICK is visible in shadow some way upstage of her. A further light beams down on her, falling from right to left. She holds out her arms slightly, pods in one hand, bowl in the other, and turns her face to the light, eyes closed, begins to smile, and holds herself there. After a while the light thickens, and rain falls lightly at a slant to her. She laughs lightly for a little, silently. MOTHER goes off right, previous lighting returns. MICK smooths the body of the fiddle, looks at the dust on his fingers.

MICK: There's varnish on her still, under the cake of mildew and paw-prints there's a shine on the old creature. You could play this and be young. Young and be still in your heart's kindness, young as a white potato in the drill, a new spud for the pot or the pit, for to give a man and his brother life. Now they kill brothers in policemen's quarters, they bring them out into a yard among the back buildings. I've heard this as clearly as a badly bowed tune, as clear as an ill dream or a clatter of rain. They ask the brothers in for questions, clean out their pockets and their toothbrushes, brought in in expectation of a long night of asking and telling, strip them down gently, picture them, and beat them. The brothers are old enough, one belly a bit fat, sagging under the ugly lights. They are beating the brothers under the lamps, the older one, the heavy old one buckling, what distance those legs have traipsed, buckling, at the belt of a whittled stick, a stick to answer promptly. Buckling in the light, in a hard time, to make you stop and think — 'Sweet life', you are thinking, 'Sweet life', everything of value is your brother, your tobaccos and papers and talks, your dreams, your hope held up as a poor cloth for protection and secrecy. So the old brother goes down to the gravel ground, a thing to watch with a bloody look, his blood in your eyes. The brother goes down, buried in his own messes, and you return to the gates of the prison alone. Nothing, no fiddle full of early days and boys' legs cavorting like goats, can bring him back. I think then, thanks for my old sleeping brother, unbeaten, as quiet as an owl in our house here on a hill above a new flood. Let me stand between him and all harms, all human harms, if no one better's to be found.

5.

As before, But MICK is now centrestage. The bright green and yellow bush lights, as with JOSEY and the GIRL before, form around him. The GIRL approaches, not looking at MICK. MICK steps into her path, and stoops towards her. The GIRL is staring, not seeing, at his chin, stalled.

MICK: Did you ever see a brown trout in a deep, muddy hole? You did not. But he is there. *(getting more and more severe)* Did you ever see a chick turn in his egg, in the liquid? You did not. Did you ever see the bladder of a mare, as she stalls in the fields, hindlegs splayed, and thrashes a pillar of piss on the grass? You could not have.

GIRL: Out of my path and let me home.

MICK: Did you ever admire the look of a white slug on a fresh young cabbage, plucked from the leaf and set down on the wooden draining board, did you ever come out in the morning and find the world of your farm stitched and corded with trails, snails' journeys that have no rhyme or reason? Did you never play foot-the-ball as a child and step on a snail, and hear the wet crunch, and curse yourself? Did you never see your father take up a tiny pup, and put its tail in his mouth, and bite it off, blood trailing down his chin?

GIRL: Out of my path and let me home.

MICK: Did you ever rise to the bait of a cornergirl, get confused in a town by cries and accounts and askings, did you never feel the trouble of a girl as she walked in front of you, agitating her skirts, making her bottom stick? Did you not, indeed? Were you never mocked, giggled at and ruffled, did you never carry your shame into an alley-way, and cry for yourself, hugging your jacket? Did you never sweat in the summer dark, did you never lie in dirty sheets, gripping yourself like a lever you could use to drive out along ploughland, did you never hear a priesteen tell you that girls had no yen for anything, no moisture, no need, no cry, no thoughts? You did not. Did you never have to stop in the street crippled by your own blood, your poker jammed in your trouser-leg, in such a manner as was plain to the every passer? You could not have. Did you never pray under soaking leaves, and wipe warm, white seeds in a cloth of jelly off your gansey? Did you never smell your own stinking perfumes, feel your body constrict in a queer mess, did you never ask the sky for a girl to hold your shoulders, stroke your forehead, say something to you you could store up for a hundred times? Did you never look in your pantry of sweet remarks and find it ever bare — bare in boyhood, barer in manhood, barest in first old age? You did not.

GIRL: Out of my path and let me home.

MICK: Do you think we are not princes, Josey and me on the hill? Do you think he could not honour you? Do you think he would always knock you on the track? Do you think he has been taught anything? Do you not see the gentle cogs in him? Do you not hear his engine whirring gently? Do you not see a moon in each of his eyes, brown eyes without whites or pupils? Do you not see a creature that would care for you? He would walk over every townland telling farmers of you, if he only knew how to do it. Do you think all the talk he has heard in his school, in the roads, in the lanes, on the gates of farms, has anything to do with him? Do you not think it is just a crust, a dirt on him, that you could wipe off if you knew the trick of it, and discover under it the house of the cleanest snail? Do you not see that, if he was unsuitable, I would do, as much for you as himself, if you were generous, and could see me in this matter?

GIRL: Out of my path and let me home.

Then, in her own light, her face turned away from MICK.

His mother was a bad speaker. A rat stole her tongue. She was hard to work. She was a slave. She bore a tailor's goose, an idiot-man. The river is the better man, good for clothes and for drowning. Here goes nothing. There were lights, there were lights to find me.

6

The same, GIRL gone. The rain has stopped. JOSEY is still asleep. MICK is standing where he was with the GIRL. Now and then JOSEY whimpers in his sleep, like a dog.

MICK *(to wake him)*: Josey.

JOSEY whimpers again.

50

MICK *(walking to the stool):* Josey. You sound like Shep.

The FATHER comes on from the left, stands between them in front of the fire.

FATHER *(looking at JOSEY):* The old cretin. What use is he to you?

MICK *(not looking at FATHER but at JOSEY):* He is every use to me. He is the thing I know.

FATHER *(putting out his left hand and taking a toothbrush from MICK's breast pocket):* What do you carry this for?

MICK: In case someone might think us uncivilised.

FATHER: And do you use the item much?

MICK *(thinking, then after a bit):* A great deal.

JOSEY *(waking, at which FATHER goes off left):* Warm. My heavens on earth.

MICK: What is it?

JOSEY: I dreamt something.

MICK: You'll toss all night in the bed, sleeping down here like that.

JOSEY: Old men may dream.

MICK: What class of a dream was it?

JOSEY: I have not the least remembrance of it. It was water though. There were lamps. Lamps of a pony-and-trap, not a car. The old high lamps, brass lamps, stuck up on poles that pony-and-traps had. If there was ever a beautiful contraption in this valley, it was a pony-and-trap. *(he wipes his face in his hands)* Well.

MICK: It's dark night. Do you want to go up?

To the left, a circle of light around the MOTHER, where she was sitting before, kneading the clay around the roots of a geranium in a clay pot. MICK steps back towards her light, and settles on the ground a little away from her, watching what she is doing.

MICK: Mam.

The MOTHER looks up briefly.

MICK: How's Mam?

The MOTHER nods at him, pressing the clay still.

MICK: There's a very strange trick in the town now.

She looks at him.

MICK: No, there is, there is. I'll tell you. I was down there after school. A few of the lads were talking about the new contraption they've set up for the sake of Moran's Meeting Rooms. So I went in myself for the mischief. It was a most unusual thing. It's like a beer mug with a lid, but it's big and white, and under the lid there's a seat for your backside.

The MOTHER stops kneading and raises her fist to him, smiling.

MICK: Well, there is. I can't help that.

The MOTHER encourages him with her forehead.

A big thing enough. I was marvelling at it. It was filled with water, you'd think it was for drinking out of, or washing your paws, the water was so clean.

MOTHER laughs silently.

You see, Mam, you're to regard this contraption as a sort of quiet spot, like a clay pit.

MOTHER looks at flowerpot, nods.

It was a marvel, the clearness of the water, and what they expected you to do in it. I wouldn't have pissed in it for the world.

MOTHER shushes him briefly, laughs.

MICK walks back to where he was, while MOTHER goes off left. Previous lighting.

JOSEY: Give us a time here still with ourselves. We've not much on, have we? Will you bury the spuds tomorrow?

MICK: They're in.

JOSEY: Fair dues.

MICK: I don't know. I went through the leg of the dog doing it.

JOSEY: Where? Over by the whitethorn?

MICK: You shouldn't bury animals in good earth. You'd no marker nor other stone to tell me. You put him in there because the soil was soft from last year's pit. It was less work for you. But a potato pit is not a grave, man.

JOSEY: He'll salt the spuds for us.

MICK: I filled him in again and dug afresh.

JOSEY: Fair dues. *(he strokes back his hair)* I was tired and dry earlier.

MICK: Jesus Christ.

JOSEY: How, Jesus Christ? A lovely man he was, with a skirt.

MICK: I'm stymied. I'm like a bullock stuck in a bog. I feel that if I move again, I'll never be contented.

JOSEY: What do you mean? On the floor there, stymied,

do you mean?

MICK: Stymied.

JOSEY: You were always stymied, weren't you? Stymied was your tune.

MICK: Aye. There's no sense in me.

JOSEY: There's only a very little. You are almost a half-wit.

MICK: The pot and the kettle.

JOSEY: Are you asleep? You have the room troubled.

MICK: I should have gone down to the town tonight. I'm not myself.

JOSEY: Well, you should have suited yourself. I was asleep completely. I might have slept till you came home. It's always home here.

MICK: I'll go out and walk. I'll go up to the top field a little way and look down on our roof. That helps me. I am shivering like a lamb. I must have been born in the snow.

JOSEY: Go on out. Talk to the horse for a minute. Don't fall over.

MICK: I'll go out for a little while. The starlight will do me good. I'll look at the boulders going up the back of the farm, or talk to the horse. I'll be able to see the old dun if there's a moon, or imagine it.

JOSEY: It will be muddy after the rain. Don't fall on a loose bit of ground.

MICK: If everything is dripping, I'll be content again. It is a lovely sound, the dripping bushes.

Call of stranded cattle below.

JOSEY: Sheep on a hill are best, poorer but best.

MICK: That must be some water now, in the channel.

JOSEY: Go out and see it.

7.

Outside. Dark, rush of river below. A patch of daylight grows on the threshold, showing the heap of the FATHER, lying on his side, his face turned upwards. MICK leans into the circle of daylight, bending over the figure.

FATHER *(softly)*: What's this putty in me?

MICK: How will I help you?

FATHER: When I breathe, I can feel putty moving in me, with hardship.

MICK: Will I pillow some part of you?

FATHER: It is an uncomfortable thing, being full of hard putty.

MICK: Will I warm it in my fingers?

FATHER: Go away out from me, I am not used to you.

MICK: Should I fetch something? Some other person?

FATHER: Pray for me.

MICK *(unhappily)*: What did you say?

FATHER: I said, pray for me, are you hard of hearing?

MICK: Our father who art in Heaven, let me talk to this man before it is impossible. Amen.

FATHER: That is a bad, ill-sounding prayer.

MICK: It is my prayer.

FATHER: I suppose you'd like to stamp on me?

MICK: That isn't what I want.

FATHER: Ah, go away with yourself somewhere, and let me lie.

MICK *(trying again):* Father most wayward, pray for -

FATHER: Pray for me properly, you fool!

MICK: Accept this most beautiful, most wayward father among the other fathers.

FATHER closes his eyes.

Old fisher, good-bye.

8

JOSEY, alone in the kitchen. He stands centrestage, facing the 'door'. When he talks, he talks conversationally, but with stilted gestures.

JOSEY: You might miss the travelling forge, Driscoll's, the songwriter, but there's no horses left for it. Charlie's the last man, the rare boy. You won't get a farrier to come up here now. There was a horse on every farm, sometimes two for a plough. Charlie is the last man. It will be a queer drop of water in the waterfall, I have seen that. I have seen that waterfall. There's a thing about a flood that's rarely said — it is greedy for the fields. It is a bull for them. You can't prevent it. Mick can not eat a salmon! He could not touch one. There are none now, there are none. The pigs ate them. The slurry, you know. You would want to bring the cows up here when they call. They wish it. Once a year in the flood they wish it heartily, to come up here with the two dark men. *(laughing)* We will hold Charlie to the house the winter, we will nurture him. We will bolster him, like our bolster, on the bed above. Mick sleeps in his dip! She left none. We could not have bolstered her. She died in blood, like a sheep, she was a stick, a small stick. He was ever a pleasing horse! Even from the furthest field he will come when I shout for him, he wouldn't budge for a foreigner. He has no interest in sugar. Do you want sugar in that, Mick? Don't poison it, he says! *(laughing)* He is a wise old horse, but very old. Let him stick by the house, certainly. He can pull the cart still, he enjoys himself in the shafts. I saw the loose shoe when he brought up the wood, I spotted it. *(laughs)* I can see, I can see. I saw that. He has plenty of go in him still. But he's troubled by age. Princelike. Holy. The very best. Isn't he? Brady's mare foaled him. Best. God now. He has pulled, he has pulled a host of loads, turfloads, timberloads, big sacks of grain and feed, bundles of firesticks like farmers in coats. He is too old. We must guard him. The friend.

He goes off left, the stage is empty. The length of the downstage section begins to light more brightly, putting the upstage region generally in shadow. MOTHER comes on from the left with a bowl of henseed. Clucking noises off. As she walks she flings the seed, but silently. When the 'hens', suggested by red brushstrokes of light, rush in, she seems to want to drive them back with stamps of her right foot. She is wearing a black dress. The seed that she casts is pierced and lit by sunlight, in beams from low upstage. When she reaches centrestage, JOSEY comes on after her. He is holding a dead rat by the tail.

JOSEY *(holding himself in)*: Mam, Mam.

The MOTHER glances back and then goes on casting the seed, the sunlight washing it till it falls.

JOSEY: Mam!

She turns properly and looks at him, and he raises up the rat for her inspection. She steps back a pace, and mimes for him to throw the rat away downstage. JOSEY looks at her blankly. She mimes again. He flings the rat away into the dark of the stage. She sweeps forward and places her palm on his cheek softly enough, but with almost a blow, straightens his jacket, pushes him away by the shoulder gently, turns and walks off right, casting the seed. This time no light falls through it. JOSEY looks after her. He walks a little way after her. At centrestage he lies on the ground, curls somewhat, sleeps. Darkness for a space. Light of the kitchen fire returns, and when it does, JOSEY is still on the ground, but his feet are facing us, his legs and arms spread as if he is fastened at the ankles and wrists. As he says the first word, the room darkens and a clear yellow light falls on him.

JOSEY *(quickly)*: Mick!

He pulls on his invisible bonds.

Mick!

His head goes back and he rests. He jerks suddenly at the bonds, straining his face up to look in front and to each side of him.

Ghost of God! Mick!

The GIRL comes on, as odd and dirty as before. She walks on her knees.

What is it?

She does not answer. She stops near him.

Where have you me? Am I far? Who has me tied?

GIRL: Did you ever put a buttercup under your chin and see the yellow?

JOSEY: What has me tied up? Are you going to sell me? Is it fair day now?

GIRL: Yellow, yellow. A bad colour all told.

JOSEY: Would you loosen me? I would pray for you if you could. I've no money.

GIRL: Did you ever notice how much improved the countryside is in a good summer — how the place looks very much another place? And gives you different hopes.

JOSEY: Mick has the money, you see. I don't even see my pension. The post-office gives it to him. Of course it is an ideal arrangement. I would lose it on the road back.

GIRL: It is very difficult though to understand the most of it. How you are to have hope, and then no hope, for the rest of the stint.

JOSEY: Loosen me, please. I have a great crick in my neck from this.

GIRL: Rain falling on the mass — that's what I thought. We are all here, all of us, the sinners and the saints and the mixtures, inside the wooden church, and the rain is falling on us. On the mass.

JOSEY: Can't you hear me? I was asking you many questions. Already you have answered none of them.

GIRL: We huddle in the porch. The whole townland almost in the one porch. Not much of a place if we are all there is to it. We've bred no one of any repute that I know of. It is not a world.

JOSEY: Where am I here?

The GIRL turns on her knees and starts back.

Wait now, wait now.

The GIRL stops.

GIRL *(not looking back):* Yellow, yellow. Bitter, bitter.

JOSEY: That's a nice song.

GIRL starts to go again, and goes off.

JOSEY: Wait! What has me here? *(quietly, to himself)* Tell me what keeps me.

Outside, noise of dripping and the rush of the swollen river below. There is a clear, dark, rinsed light, with high darkblue clouds crossing an otherwise lustrous night-sky. The larger kitchen window is a rectangle of brighter light, illumed by the fire inside. MICK stands with his back to us, arms at his sides, staring at the house, silent. The figure of the horse goes slowly, quietly, head down, from left to right, passing some way in front of MICK's back. After a time, JOSEY comes into the area of the 'door'. He looks at MICK, pauses on the threshold. He comes forward, places hand on MICK's shoulder, and brings him in.

10

Inside the kitchen. The stairs are again visible on the right. MICK and JOSEY stand a few feet inside the 'door'. The fire is low.

MICK *(needing help)*: Josey.

JOSEY: Christ in his Heaven.

MICK: What, Josey?

JOSEY: Mick, I dreamed I was a girl. I fell asleep on the floor.

MICK: What were you like?

JOSEY: I was miserable.

MICK: Much the same then.

JOSEY: Oh, but I was very miserable, I wanted to go in the river quick.

MICK: Dreaming. You'll have strange pains from the damp in that floor.